I DON'T LOOK LIKE WHAT I'VE BEEN THROUGH

Seven Ways to Turn your MESS into a MASTERPIECE

By: Tammi L. Durden

ROYSTON
Publishing

BK Royston Publishing
P. O. Box 4321
Jeffersonville, IN 47131
502-802-5385
http://www.bkroystonpublishing.com
bkroystonpublishing@gmail.com

Cover Design: Elite Book Covers

ISBN-13: 978-1-946111-97-5

Printed in the United States of America

DEDICATION

With much gratitude and love, I first dedicate this book to my God that empowers me to write and share my message with the world. Without you, this would not be possible, and I owe you everything. Thank you for using me as your messenger.

To my daughter Ebony Durden-Peavy, I dedicate and write this book as a part of my legacy to you. Thank you for your continuous and undying love and support over the years. You are my WHY.

With sincere appreciation I dedicate this book to my publisher, Julia A. Royston that continues to push and believe in me as an author.

Finally, I dedicate this book to women across the globe that have been through the fire, but you are still standing, still pushing, and refuse to give up- this one's for you!

Table of Contents

INTRODUCTION

So…life happened, now what? There I was sitting in a pile of regret, about to start my next pity party. All in one fell swoop I lost my business, my husband, my homes, my car, and my friends. Once the smoke cleared, it was just me, my daughter, and a big pile of debt. I had fallen down a slippery slope and couldn't seem to grab hold of anything to break the fall and pull myself back up.

Did I ask for trouble to knock on my door and stalk me? Of course not. But ever since my tsunami of setbacks had come and gone, I just wasn't the same. To be honest with you, I let myself go. I lost focus and my confidence, so my entire image suffered.

If I could venture back even further, I grew up with low self-esteem. I never thought I was good enough, smart enough, pretty enough, or talented enough. I constantly looked for people to validate, accept or simply like me. It took many years and a lot of costly mistakes to overcome this. But I learned and applied the lessons. After identifying my true worth in my mid-twenties, I finally felt good about myself. When you know better, you do better.

You see, life happens to the best of us, but the good news is you don't have to park there. What did not kill you strengthened you. Moving from Mess to Masterpiece begins as an inside job that spills over to the outside. It's not just about purchasing a new wardrobe or getting a makeover. There has to be some internal work done to produce the desired result.

A total transformation must take place. There must be balance. This is a process that engages Mind, Body, and Spirit. You don't have to look stressed out, worn out, or broken down. How you show up in the world matters and the overall success and outcome of your life depends on it.

So, the big question is, "How does this transformation happen"?

…after you've experienced a daunting illness…

...after you've gone through the ugly divorce...

...after you've experienced violent abuse for years...

...after you've hit rock bottom and lost everything...

It begins with healing from your past and getting a new vision for your life. You must be intentional about bringing a positive shift in your life. Insanity is defined as doing the same thing over and over but expecting different results. You've got to do something different to get different results.

In fact, looking like what you have gone through only prolongs the journey. When you look like you just went through a divorce, it's going to be even harder to find the new love you are looking for. When you look like your business is failing, it's going to be even harder to get new clients. When you look like you just lost your job who will want to hire you? It's time to level up.

That's where this book comes into play. Purposefully positioned on every page are the tools, strategies, and solutions that will aid you in moving your life from Mess to Masterpiece and to get the results that you have been searching for. This inspiring and insightful reading is sure to catapult your entire being to the next dimension. Keep an open mind, a receptive spirit and apply the principles. When doing so, you are sure to encounter a true metamorphosis in your life. The journey begins now...

CHAPTER 1: BE GRACIOUS

Give yourself a break!

I believe that we are the best examples of how other people should treat us. If we don't respect or be kind to our own selves, how can we expect others to treat us well? When considering the meaning of the word gracious, I have found that it means to be courteous, kind, and pleasant. How many times have you been kind to others and treated yourself like 5-day-old leftovers pushed to the back of the refrigerator?

We ignore and neglect ourselves, but expect others to treat us well. Although we have to clean up our messes, we shouldn't tear ourselves down in the process. Sometimes we are our own worst critics. Why do we beat ourselves up so much? We say things to ourselves like:

- ❖ I'm so stupid!
- ❖ Why did you do that dummy?
- ❖ You were such a fool to trust him.
- ❖ Can't you get anything right?
- ❖ I'm such a loser!

The list goes on and on. The fact of the matter is none of us gets it right 100% of the time. There are enough critics in the world to beat up on us, so why attack ourselves? Remember, your words matter and can determine your very existence.

Give yourself a break!

You messed up, right? Maybe it was your fault and you could have made some better choices and decisions. The good news is that your mistakes did not derail your destiny. No matter what it looks like, it's not over and you still have a shot at living your best life!

Several years ago, when I was a single mother, I was extremely protective of my daughter and was very careful of the male influences that I allowed her to be exposed to. I didn't bring men home because I wanted to keep her safe. Finally, after years of being single, I decided to get married for the SECOND time. This time would be forever, I thought. I married a preacher at my father's church! I was sure my daughter would be safe around him. For the first few years everything seemed to go well. We worked together in ministry, owned a successful business, a nice home, as well as a couple of rental properties. Then the unthinkable happened…in the middle of the night, my husband attempted to molest my daughter. I will never forget that night. The panic, screams, and tears of my daughter will be forever embedded in my memory. It shook me to my core.

For years I was tormented with this, placing total blame on myself for what happened. I constantly questioned and made statements such as:

- ❖ How could I let such a horrible thing happen?

- ❖ Maybe if I didn't work so many long hours at the office, I could have seen this coming.
- ❖ Was I not paying attention to the signs?
- ❖ I should have investigated more into his background before marrying him.
- ❖ Was I not good enough as a wife?
- ❖ I failed my daughter.
- ❖ I didn't protect her.

I can't tell you how many times this replayed over and over in my mind. I even slipped into a state of depression for a while. I just couldn't seem to let it go. This was taking me on an emotional roller coaster that was reeling out of control. I was in serious trouble.

Finally, I decided to get some help. I had already made sure my daughter saw a therapist, but I needed professional assistance as well. By the way, there is no shame in getting help. Often, we carry around baggage of the past because we are too embarrassed or prideful to see someone. At this point for me it was Existing vs. Living...Life or Death...and I chose to get help and Live!

Here's what I learned: Being gracious to yourself can involve several things including **Self-love, Forgiveness, and Self-worth.**

SELF-LOVE

Self-love is so important to our overall living and well-being. It impacts how you deal with problems, whom you choose to marry, and ultimately the personal image that you project to others.

So, you are probably wondering, what exactly is self-love? Well, in a nutshell, self-love is appreciating and accepting yourself for who you are. It is not merely feeling good after buying a new outfit or reading a great book that inspired you. But it is how you feel about yourself at the end of the day with everything on the table...the good...the bad...and the ugly. It involves embracing and loving every quirk, asset, imperfection, and the uniqueness of YOU.

Are any of us perfect? Of course, the answer to that question is NO. Will we ever be perfect? The answer remains the same, NO. The important thing to keep in mind is, although we are a continual work in progress, it is imperative that we discover self-love right where we are. You see, we tend to tear ourselves down because of the mistakes that we've made in the past such as:

- ❖ That toxic relationship that we should have walked away from years ago, but chose to stay in
- ❖ Continually overeating and gaining so much weight until our health began to pay the price for it
- ❖ Not finishing college and failing to get a degree

Choose to focus on your strengths and not your weaknesses. Know that this is an ever-evolving process that expands and matures us as individuals. As we grow, there's less room for criticism, more room for compassion, and no room for self-destruction.

Self-love is more powerful than you think. Those who truly practice this way of being tend to be clear about their purpose and know what they want. Remember, the more you love yourself the better you can love others.

FORGIVENESS

Whew! This can be a tough one. Forgiveness requires facing the truth of your situation head on and being brave enough to deal with it. Some situations can be so heart-wrenching that it feels like you will never recover. Just know that the key to your recovery is forgiveness.

The thing about forgiveness is that the person it benefits most is you. Many of us have held on for years to past offenses, hurts, and experiences that are eating away at our lives. This has to stop. As human beings, we were not designed to exist this way.

Forgiveness jump-starts the healing process, and it begins with forgiving yourself first. No matter how many times you failed and for every poor choice you've made…give yourself a break! You may have messed up, but life doesn't stop here. The simple fact that you are still living and breathing means that you have been given another chance. So, take full advantage of this opportunity and live!

Not only should you forgive yourself, but also forgive those that have hurt or offended you. Trust me, I know it's hard. But remember, this is for you. If you want to move forward and live your best life you've got to let it go.

I was once in a relationship with a gentleman. Keep in mind this is after experiencing two bad marriages and divorces. At this point I just wanted to have a great relationship and be happy. Have you ever felt that way? I thought that if I was honest and upfront by sharing my past experiences with this guy and how I had been hurt before in relationships, he would understand and not engage in the same behavior. I assumed that if I laid everything on the table at the beginning of the relationship, we would both be clear of certain expectations and know our boundaries. This was not the case. Of course, initially things seemed to be going well. Then, little by little, I began to see signs of things shifting in a different direction. But, of course, I chose to ignore the signs, thinking things would magically change without any intervention or conversation. I turned my head to the obvious and did not address the issues. As a result, this guy cheated on me and had a baby with another woman. I was devastated.

For a long time, I held unforgiveness in my heart towards him. When I heard his voice, someone called his name, or I saw a picture of him, I cringed. Deep down inside, I knew that if I was going to get past this and move on to live a healthy and happy life, I had to forgive. I had to heal. Not only was it important for me to forgive him, but I also had to forgive myself for what I allowed to happen. This is what jump-started the healing process for me and will for you as well. Forgive to heal, and you will love yourself for doing so.

SELF-WORTH

A catchy phrase that I hear is, "Know your worth." What does that really mean? Let's take a closer look. **Self-worth** essentially is the opinion and value you place on yourself. For example, do you feel like you deserve good things to happen for you? Do you believe that you are a good or bad person? Are you enough?

Your self-worth is the catalyst for your choices and decisions. It determines if you play big or small in life, whether or not you step out of your comfort zone, or if you decide to settle for less than what is available to you. If you don't think you are enough, you will never reach for greater.

Listen, if the truth be told, it doesn't matter how badly you messed up in the past, or what horrible mistakes you made, or even the poor choices you settled on. Somehow, some way, always find value in yourself. At the end of the day, you are still worthy of God's best for your life.

For a long time in my life, I did not value myself. I grew up with low self-esteem. Dating all the way back to elementary school, I looked for others to like me...validate me...accept me...and love me. I tried my best to fit in and be a part of the cliques and popular circles, but it never seemed to work. As a result of years of looking for love in all the wrong places, I became pregnant at the age of 15 and gave birth to my daughter at 16. Yes, I was a teenage mom, and it was scary!

I will be honest with you—I did not value myself for a long while, and I was in my twenties by the time I finally got it. I realized that I was truly special and had a lot to offer. I decided that if no one else would appreciate that I was an amazing person with a lot to offer, I would find the value in myself and be good with that.

The other thing that helped me in this time was to surround myself with people that celebrated me instead of just tolerating me. I cannot tell you how important it is to have positive individuals around you that believe in you and have your best interest at heart. This simply reinforces what you already know to be true.

We are human…we all make mistakes. Sometimes we just don't get it right. So, give yourself a big hug, and no matter what, always remember this:

Be Kind To You!

Forgive You!

Appreciate You!

Give Yourself A Break!

✓ **Transformational Tip:** Stop being angry and resentful towards yourself for past offenses and mess-ups. They are just a part of life. The longer you wallow in past failures and mistakes, the longer you miss out on the phenomenal life that is ahead of you.

CHAPTER 2: BE POWERFUL

Know your truth and stand in your power

As you transition from Mess to Masterpiece, one thing you must be totally convinced of is that you are powerful. I know, at times you don't feel very powerful, but you really are. When you've been blindsided by life and everything is a mess, it can be challenging to gather up enough strength just to face the next day. You see, I've been there, so I get it.

The key is to identify YOUR truth—not what people have said about you, not what your current situation is, not what happened to you in the past, but the thing that is constant and real in your life no matter the circumstances. Who are you? What are your values and beliefs? You must know this and have an unshakable confidence in who you are. Don't allow what happened in the past to dictate your future.

You may ask the question: "How do I stand in my power when I feel so weak?" Simply put, power is the ability to be effective as who you are. So, when you stand in your power, you take seriously the morals, values, and principles that are important to you without wavering. Essentially you are fully persuaded of who you are, what you can do, and why you do it. This is your power...this is your truth.

When you stand in your power, it does not require a lot of fanfare, noise, or attention. There is a quiet strength that exudes from you that doesn't have to be heard or seen in order to establish the very being of who you are. Real power comes from within and doesn't need an introduction or announcement when you enter the room. It is just a natural, unspoken force and a part of who you are. You've outlasted some tough times, and as a result, your power and presence speak for themselves.

Particularly as females we bear a lot of things and wear many different hats. We are mom, wife, chauffer for the kids, ministry leader, daughter, best friend, CEO, sister, chef, confidant, volunteer, and the list goes on and on. I believe sometimes we amaze ourselves with how we seem to hold it together and get it all done. This is where that real power kicks in. We were built to be strong and designed to withstand the most challenging situations. Whether you know it or not, every setback that you have overcome has made you more powerful.

We were all born and created with a certain degree of power that is submerged deep within. But don't be deceived; there is a greater source of power that we must draw on. Accessing that power and staying connected is what will keep you on top. This can be accomplished through consistent prayer and meditation.

May I offer a word of caution? In order to consistently stand in your power, always remember to keep your cup full. What I'm saying is, you can't give and give until you are depleted and expect to still be effective. Remember, power is the ability to be effective. Once your cup is empty, you have nothing left to give, nor do you have anything reserved for yourself. In this state you are no good for yourself or anyone else. Learn to protect your power. Fill yourself up and keep your cup full to running over. What's inside the cup is for you and the overflow is what you can share with others. Be careful as some people will receive from you but never give back. Handle your power wisely.

One of the biggest enemies to your power is people-pleasing. Why do we feel compelled to satisfy people? Unfortunately, we don't value who we are and suppress our true worth in fear of what others may think. Stop it! When you yield to this type of behavior, you surrender your position.

From childhood to adulthood, I can't tell you how many countless hours I spent trying to please people. Fitting in was what I wanted so badly. I figured if I could make enough people happy and do what they wanted, then I would be liked and included in the various circles and cliques. Well, things did not work out as I planned. Honestly, after giving gifts and doing tons of favors for people, I still ended up lonely, used, and depleted both emotionally and financially. They received what they wanted, but I was empty. When all was said and done, I couldn't blame them. I chose to surrender to people-pleasing, and these were the consequences that I suffered for it.

Don't give up your power. Refuse to shrink back. Everyone will not like you, but that's okay. Stand in your power and make no apologies for who you are. Be bold, be beautiful, be you.

THREE WAYS TO ERADICATE PEOPLE-PLEASING:

Set Boundaries

When it comes to eliminating people-pleasing from your life, it is important to set boundaries. You don't always have to say yes to every invitation or agree with everyone else's opinion. There are certain conversations that you may not need to be a part of. Kindly decline and walk away. It doesn't matter if they accept you or not, you are powerful all by yourself. No one has to validate you, accept you, or affirm you. In and of yourself you are powerful. Know how far you are willing to go in any given situation, and hold to that standard without wavering.

Be the Boss of You

In other words, don't let other people control your decisions. Have clarity of thought and be decisive. Base your choices on your own personal values and beliefs. At the end of the day, you must be happy with the course of action that you take. Don't get me wrong, it's okay to ask for suggestions, ideas, and get sound advice from others. However, don't ever feel as though you must compromise to do what others think is best for you. In most cases, individuals that try to manipulate and control your life have no control of their own lives, so it's easier for them to place the attention on "fixing" your problems.

Stop Playing the Comparison Game

I've seen so many times where we cheat ourselves from living our best lives by constantly making a comparison to others. Comparison diminishes your power and makes you feel inferior. There will always be someone smarter than you, better than you, or wealthier than you. The important thing is to be the very best YOU that you can be. Besides, things are not always as they appear. Behind the scenes, some of the people you are comparing yourself to may have your same struggles.

When I was a kid, some of the older ladies in my church would compare one girl to another and say, "You should be more like her." Habitual comparison is never healthy. It eats away at your power little by little, and before you know it, you are left with nothing but low self-esteem. When you are tempted to compare yourself and your journey to others, press the pause button and begin to appreciate where you are now and the obstacles you had to overcome to be standing in your current space. You are powerful. Own it and refuse to play the comparison game.

Remember, when you stand in your power, there is an inner knowing that all is well, and you are confident that everything is working for your good. It is vitally important to be clear about your priorities and intentions. Always believe in and stay true to yourself, without wavering or compromising. Continually strive to be the very best that you can be, regardless of your circumstances. Even if at times you falter, know that every failure and setback will make you stronger. Despite what you've been through, you are still here, still standing, and still winning. You are powerful!

✓ **Transformational Tip:** Surround yourself with people that appreciate your gifts. Be discerning. Everyone that's with you is not for you, and you can't please them all, so don't waste your time trying.

CHAPTER 3: BE POSITIVE

The power of a positive attitude

In a world that seems to be filled with so much negativity, sometimes it is a struggle to be positive. Whether you're on the job or just watching the daily news, the cancer of negativity seems to ooze in and take residence.

One critical key that I've discovered on this journey from Mess to Masterpiece is the power of a positive attitude. Your attitude is your way of thinking that is also reflected as a part of your behavior. The saying, "Your attitude determines your altitude," is so true. Whether it is in your career or in relationships, your attitude will decide the extent of your elevation.

When you are positive, that means you must entertain good thoughts. This positivity contributes to your sense of personal power and creates a zest and excitement for life! Having a positive attitude is a choice—it's all in the state of mind. Everything originates with a thought and flows outward. Having the proper mindset and ways of thinking is paramount. If you continually find yourself in a negative state, begin to ask yourself questions like: What's on my mind that is causing me to feel so terrible? Why am I always in such a bad mood?

What I've found is many times we relive the past and continue to replay that same old movie of how we were hurt, wronged, used, and abused. Please understand that I am not discounting anyone's horrific experiences, because I've been there myself. However, this type of thought pattern breeds negativity and low-level thinking.

After husband number two and I separated, to be totally honest, I was bitter. I resented him for everything he had done to my daughter and myself. I despised him for all the lies that he told and all the deception that had taken place. Because he was a minister, I held him to a higher standard. I thought he would be our protector, but he turned out to be our predator. As a result, for a long time I begrudged male ministers and pastors because I refused to let go of what happened in my marriage. Yes, this bad attitude manifested itself in my actions, hindered my recovery, and impacted the lives of those around me. I had to let it go.

Will you feel like being positive all the time? Probably not, but if you can practice positivity most of the time it will greatly benefit your transformation process. **Here are a few ways that you can consistently maintain a positive attitude:**

❖ **Start your day with finding something positive to focus on.** Maybe a promotion you received on your job, meeting a new friend, or making that new sale in your business! This could also be accomplished by listening to a motivational message or reading a page from a great book. Be sure to guard your ear gate and monitor your thoughts. Keep it positive!

❖ **Do something good for someone else.** What I've found is when you shift the attention from yourself and choose to be kind and helpful to someone else, it puts you in a positive state of mind. You will find that making someone else's day is rewarding.

❖ **Appreciate your current state.** Although things may not be optimal in your life right now, look at what you've been through and what you've overcome. You are still standing, and it didn't take you out. Things could be a whole lot worse.

❖ **Practice the power of a smile.** Even in the most difficult environments, choose to wear a smile. Most times when you smile at someone they will smile back. This helps set the tone and atmosphere to be one that is warm and inviting. You never know what others are going through, and that one smile can make the difference in their day.

❖ **Keep a positive circle.** Surrounding yourself with positive people is very likely to help you stay on track and contribute to your personal growth and development.

Being positive is a lifestyle. Remember, like attracts like. If you want to attract more positive things into your life, YOU must be positive. When you decide to practice positivity, everyone will not be on board with it. When you walk into the break room at work, Negative Nancy will still try to lure you into her morning cup of negativity, but don't fall for it. Resist the temptation to let other people's negativity bring you down. Refrain from speaking bad things about others. This only feeds into a negative attitude. Practice being happy for some else's success, celebrate with them, and truly mean it from your heart.

As you continue with your transformation, it is important to release negative energy and become a source of goodness that lifts the spirits of those around you. As human beings, we have a certain energetic structure. Our emotions are energy that ultimately impacts our vibration. In other words, your vibration level is lowered by negative feelings. On the other hand, your vibration level is elevated by positive feelings. The energy that you carry is so important. It can make or break your success in your career, relationships, and every area of your life. Everything you engage in is a result of the energy you present. I'm sure you've heard the term "positive vibes." You see it on t-shirts and across social media: #positivevibes. No one really wants to be around a big ball of negativity that brings them down. Only positive energy attracts more positive energy.

From a physical standpoint, negative energy depletes you of your liveliness and overall well-being. On the other hand, positive energy revitalizes you and maintains a degree of joy and good health in your life. The consequences for holding on to negative energy can be detrimental.

The moment you walk into a room, people can pick up on your energy. If it's not good, most times people will avoid contact with you. This is how jobs are lost, long-lasting friendships end, and marriages fail. You see, a negative attitude is contagious and can spread like wildfire. It becomes toxic and eats away at anything in its path. If you find that you are stuck in a negative abyss, sometimes getting an accountability partner can help.

Finally, let's talk about the power of the spoken word. Do you know that your words have power? My favorite book, The Bible, says in Proverbs 18:21, "The tongue has the power of life and death, and those who love it will eat its fruit." You have the power to speak things into existence. Why not use those words to speak positive things into your life? Begin to honor and affirm yourself daily with positive statements such as:

- ❖ I am beautiful
- ❖ I am brilliant
- ❖ I am amazing
- ❖ I am powerful
- ❖ I am enough

Use your words for good and not harm. Resist the temptation to complain and look at the bad side of things. The more you speak positive words over your life, the better you will feel about yourself, and you will begin to attract the wonderful things you desire.

✓ **Transformational Tip:** The more bad things you say, the more bad things you are calling into your life. Always be sure to monitor your mouth, your mind, and your motives.

CHAPTER 4: BE GRATEFUL

Gratitude opens the door for better

I know, you are probably saying, "Tammi, how can I be grateful when I look around at the MESS I'm in?" Some of you are probably looking at the aftermath of your situation and wondering how a MASTERPIECE can ever be created from such a major disruption in life.

That's just it. The chaos and calamity come to make something meaningful and impactful in your life that can ultimately be a blessing to someone else. The Bible tells us in 1 Thessalonians 5:18, "Be thankful in all circumstances...." In other words, whether it is in the middle of your mess or after the smoke has cleared, if you survived and are still here, give thanks.

Let's talk about what it means to be grateful. Being thankful and showing appreciation are what gratefulness is all about. It is not contingent on the condition of your circumstances. You know, it's easy to have a thankful heart when everything is going well. The challenge comes when all hell breaks loose...what do you do then? How is your attitude now? Do you find yourself complaining about everything? Tread lightly in this area because the reality is things could always be a lot worse, so be thankful for what you have and where you are in life.

To be honest, in the worst of situations there is always something to be grateful for. It is simply up to us to find it and focus on the good. Will it be easy? Most times it is not, but in order to see your situation turn around and have more good things flow into your life, it is imperative to practice gratitude. If you can push past the mess and be grateful, you will see that you are one step away from your next level. Let's look at pushing past the mess.

I created an acronym for the word:

M ISTAKES

E XCUSES

S ETBACKS

S TAGNANCY

<u>MISTAKES</u>

The reality is we've all made mistakes in life, some big and some small, but making mistakes is inevitable because we are human beings. At some point we will produce actions that result in error or failure. It's just a part of life. The beauty about mistakes is that they always come to teach you a lesson that you would not have otherwise learned. That's the key—learn the lesson and apply it in your life so that you don't make the same mistake again.

I was in business several years ago after transitioning from my "good job" to owning my own business as a single mother. We had some lean days in the beginning. Once I got my feet on the ground as a mortgage broker, I began to recruit loan officers to come on board with me. Business was booming! Eventually I did not have to originate my own loans, but simply oversee operations. At one point, a successful and more experienced mortgage broker offered to mentor me. I kindly declined. This was probably one of the biggest MISTAKES that I made with this business. You see, I was in business for myself and by myself. I did not have a mentor, coach, or professional accountability partner. Maybe if I'd had a mentor, I would have been guided to pay more attention to the shift in the market and position my business accordingly. In hindsight, I discovered when saying no to her offer, I forfeited the potential to grow, expand, and possibly still be in business today. Big mistake.

So, I had to make a decision. Do I continue to hold on to past mistakes, or do I learn from them, grow from them, and move forward? You see, when you remain tied to your past mistakes, you tend to become bitter and not better. There's a quote by

Bishop T. D. Jakes that says, "When you hold on to your history, you do it at the expense of your destiny."

My questions for you:

❖ What past mistakes are you holding on to?
❖ What failure are you allowing to stop you from healing from your past?
❖ What mess-up is blocking your gratitude?

Whether you married the wrong person once or even twice…

Maybe you compromised your truth just to fit in…

It could have been mistakes you made in your career or business that cost you everything…

I can't say this enough. It happened, learn the lesson from it, and choose to grow with gratitude.

EXCUSES

Excuses are the crutches of the uncommitted and gratitude blockers. A negative connotation is usually associated with excuses. For example:

- ❖ I'm too old
- ❖ I don't have enough money
- ❖ I need a degree
- ❖ They don't like me
- ❖ I'm not connected to the right people

Excuses, Excuses, Excuses!

I often ask the question, despite your past experiences, and if money were no object, would you live your wildest dream? Would that put you in a state of gratitude? With whatever gifts, talents, and resources that you have right now, why not use them to make some level of progress and be thankful that you have something of value to work with?

You see, the more we use excuses to justify and defend our shortcomings, the more negative opportunities we invite into our lives, and the longer we stay in our mess. When you opt to be thankful no matter what state you are in, negativity and excuses have no place in that space.

SETBACKS

If you are reading this book and have been living on this earth for any amount of time, most likely you have experienced some type of setback. The fact of the matter is life happens, and it happens to the best of us. It doesn't discriminate, but it comes for us all. Whether it is a natural disaster, divorce, sickness, abuse, or loss of a loved one...life happens.

I know what you are probably thinking...it's easier said than done to push past setbacks and be grateful. When you've experienced so much hurt, pain, and disappointment, you may wonder how there could possibly be a silver lining in this. The thing you should know is your setback is just a set-up for your next level of success. Although it never feels good during the process, every challenge you overcome should make you a better person. If you can push past the mess your best days are ahead of you.

As a pastor's kid born and raised in the church, I always tried to be a good person and do the right thing. I fell short many times but did my best. When I experienced my tsunami of setbacks (divorce, failed business, bankruptcy, foreclosure, car repossession, and depression), I was distraught, lost, and broken. It never occurred to me that one of the outcomes of this horrible disaster would be me writing my first book, "Get Up, Dust Yourself Off And Win!" I've also had the opportunity to positively impact lives across the globe with this message in written, electronic, and audiobook formats, and through personal appearances.

What if I had elected to settle in my mess, remain stuck in the past, and despise the setback? We must recognize that what we go through is merely a refining process that will catapult us to greater if we embrace it, see the good, and be thankful.

STAGNANCY

Stagnancy occurs after you hold on to the mistakes, wallow in your excuses, and stay stuck in your past. Often traumatized by the negative experiences we've encountered and the fear of being hurt again, we retreat and hide behind the pain. As a result, there's no movement or progression in your life. Have you been here before? I certainly have. This is what happens when you refuse to take on an attitude of gratitude but stay safely tucked away in your comfort zone.

Although you may not be where you want to be right now, be grateful for who you are becoming. Take a chance on life again! Once you shift into a position of gratitude, this will promote positive momentum in your life that will transition you from where you are to where you want to be.

Remember, gratitude opens the door for better. It is an attitude of the heart. Be thankful for what you have right now and the experiences you've had, whether good or bad. Try incorporating a gratitude journal into your daily success habits. Every day in your journal, list three things that you are grateful for. You can do this first thing in the morning or at night before going to bed. This daily exercise of focusing on gratitude will revolutionize your perspective and begin to attract more good things into your life.

✓ **Transformational Tip:** Turn your Mess into a Masterpiece by taking on a grateful and resilient spirit to find the good in your misfortunes.

CHAPTER 5: BE OPEN

Opportunities don't always come packaged as you expect

Being open largely has to do with your mindset. It involves welcoming new opportunities, different people, and the possibility of experiencing something that you haven't before. Keeping an open mind can be a challenge, but it will also prove to be extremely rewarding. Closed-mindedness and limiting beliefs can cause you to miss out on promising opportunities. There are some things that have been orchestrated just for you, but if you are not open to receiving them, they will never manifest in your life. Have you heard the saying, "A closed mouth doesn't get fed"? Well, a closed mind doesn't either.

I used to be totally against traveling internationally. It all boiled down to fear. I convinced myself that if I left the U.S. and traveled abroad, there was a possibility that a war would break out and I would not be able to return home. For years I held on tightly to this limiting belief and blocked any opportunities to travel internationally. Then, I met a colleague at work that was not only courageous enough to travel across the globe, but she often traveled alone. This blew my mind! I began to listen to her countless stories of places she had visited, and sometimes she shared photographs of her amazing escapades. Little by little I began to entertain thoughts of traveling to places like Australia, London, New Zealand, Paris, and Africa. At that time, I did not realize that I had a global calling on my life to speak and write to other nations. The more I became open to the possibility, I began to attract opportunities to travel abroad into my life. A few years later, I received an invitation to speak in London at a conference. I shudder when I think about if I had not allowed myself to be exposed to greater. This clearly would have hindered my purpose and robbed me of my destiny. There's a cost to pay for not having an open mind. I am so grateful that I opted to upgrade my thinking.

The key element that determines your success is mindset. What you consistently think about directly impacts your behavior. In order to achieve the success that you want in life, you must master your mind. Dismiss any and all limiting beliefs that are lingering in your thought life. Failing to do so will keep you stuck and stagnant. One of my favorite quotes in The Bible is Proverbs 23:7, which says, "For as he thinks in his heart, so is he." In other words, you become what you think about. So, if you really want to see positive transformation in your life, it requires a positive mindset.

Now I will be honest with you, keeping an open mind can be one of the toughest things to practice, but in order to shift from Mess to Masterpiece, it is necessary. Being open exposes you to vulnerability.

This can appear to be risky, especially if you are a private person. However, to create new experiences, it is crucial to motivate yourself to try new things. There's a saying that still holds true which says, "If you do what you've always done, you will get what you always have." Be willing to step out of your comfort zone and do something different. Go to new restaurants, read a new book, meet new people. Start with something small, then expand. Be open and say yes when the right opportunities present themselves.

Let me tell you about Jessica. She was smart, attractive, successful, and divorced for ten years. Although her first marriage did not last, it was Jessica's heart's desire to be married. After numerous failed attempts at dating and a series of dead-end relationships, she decided to take a break. It had been one disappointment after another, and to be honest, Jessica was beginning to lose hope. One day a friend of hers asked if she had ever tried any of the online dating services. Of course, she said no, as she had never considered this an option. Jessica felt that it was a big scam packed with lies, fake profiles, and just another way for men to take advantage of you. Besides, she was old-fashioned and believed in meeting men the traditional way. After hearing a few success stories that her friend shared with her, Jessica began to carefully analyze her past dating experiences and relationships that she had done "her way." Not to mention, having received a new promotion at work, she did not have time to hang out and meet new people. So, she thought, "Why not try something different?" Jessica became open to new possibilities! This was the first step to welcoming something new into her life.

Now here's the challenge with Jessica—she was accustomed to dating men that were tall, dark, and handsome. The total opposite types of men were responding to her profile. So, she had to become even more open and expand her boundaries to the possibility that her mate would not fit her ideal male profile. Well, Jessica had come this far, so she decided to be flexible and give the other guys a try. One day she finally met "the one." He was totally opposite of what she had always imagined him being. Instead of tall and dark, he was short and light. There were a few other things on her list that did not match up, but he was without a doubt the man for her. As a result of Jessica being open, she met her true love and has been happily married for eight years. This happened only because she chose to expand her mindset and be open to trying something different.

So now that you have decided to take an open approach to life, here are a few things that can help:

❖ **Ask questions**
It's okay if you don't know everything. None of us do. Never be afraid to ask questions. Often this is the only way to learn about things, and it helps you keep an open mind as you expand your knowledge base and gain a better understanding in certain areas.

❖ **Avoid secluding yourself**
Welcome the opportunity to meet new people, network, or even join a professional organization. Try something different than what you are familiar with. Be social and form new relationships.

What you will find is when you choose to expose yourself to others with a unique set of interests, this will provide fresh experiences that can change your life.

❖ **Embrace differing opinions**
Seek to understand and resist the temptation to jump to conclusions when presented with a contrasting perspective. Treat it as a learning opportunity and find the wisdom in it. Remember, everyone will not hold your same opinion. It is always a good practice to try seeing things through the other person's eyes to get a better understanding.

❖ **Fight fear and do it anyway**
Step out of your comfort zone and live! Don't allow the fear of failure to paralyze you. So, what if you've never done it before? Forget about what people may say. These are merely the pawns of fear to hold you hostage and stop you from living your best life.

Remember, opportunities don't always come packaged as you expect, so it is important to be willing to do the work it takes to maintain an open mind. Amazing new opportunities are all around you, but you must be prepared to receive them.

✓ **Transformational Tip:** Always be willing to listen and learn. Seeing things from a different perspective will keep you open to new possibilities.

CHAPTER 6: BE ATTRACTIVE

Image is everything

Have you ever had something beautiful catch your attention and stop you dead in your tracks? Maybe a lovely bouquet of flowers, a breathtaking sunset, or even a stunning human being? There was something so appealing and pleasing to the senses that captured your interest. That, my friend, is called attractiveness.

When you are attractive, you carry a certain energy and confidence that command attention. You may ask the question, "Why is being physically attractive so important?" I know, I hear you. Although people may say, "Don't judge a book by its cover," we all know that is not true. It happens every day. Your appearance matters. It ultimately determines the amount of your income, your career path, and even the attractiveness of your partner. Whether you are headed to a job interview, first date, board meeting, or Sunday morning church service, it makes a difference how you show up. At the end of the day, when you look good, you feel good. As a matter of fact, your physical presentation impacts your overall personality and how you view yourself. It gives a great boost to your self-confidence when your appearance is at its best.

Not only does your attractiveness impact how you see yourself, but it also plays a big role in how others view you. Studies show that people are biased toward those who look attractive, with study participants rating attractive people as more trustworthy, smart, entertaining, and even wealthier than those with a less attractive appearance. People tend to gravitate towards individuals that look well groomed.

I understand that you've probably had some alarming disruptions in your life that caused you not to feel attractive. As a matter of fact, having a stellar look was the furthest thing from your mind. When you are in survival mode, being attractive drops to the bottom of the list. But now that you have conquered your setbacks, it is time to turn your Mess into a Masterpiece and start showing up as a winner. Leave the pain of the past behind. Get up, clean up, and look like the greatness you were destined to be. You don't have to look like what you've been through. Your attractiveness is paramount to your overall image, and trust me, image is everything.

So, let's get clear about what image really is and its significance. Your image is the external presentation of who you are to the world. This impression begins in your mind and is projected outwardly to those around you. It is an accumulation of external messages that we broadcast, whether trying to or not, through our appearance, conversation, lifestyle, and behavior. Everything you say and do advertises something about who you are and adds to your external image.

When you walk into a room, your appearance is speaking. Before you open your mouth to say a word, you are being silently evaluated based on your outward presentation. So, my next question is, what is your image speaking to those who you encounter? Is your image communicating what you want it to say? Remember, you only get one chance to make a first impression.

In many facets of life, especially in the business world, first impressions mean everything. For example, let's say an employer received two resumes with similar education and experience, and both candidates get called in for an interview. After meeting with them both, the only difference between the two comes down to their physical presentation. Who is more likely to get the job? To be honest, there is a high probability that the candidate with the sharpest image will be the one to secure the position.

I worked for a company where I participated in conducting a panel interview. We narrowed the potential candidates down to a few individuals. All resumes, for the most part, represented what we were looking for. Based on paper no one had a significant advantage over the other. The in-person interviews would be the determining factor. About midway into the interviews, we sat in the conference room waiting on the next candidate to be escorted in. When she walked through the door, I immediately noticed that her white blouse was totally wrinkled. For a large part of the interview I could not focus on how she responded to questions, because I was distracted by the wrinkles whenever I looked at her. After the interview, most of the panel members mentioned how her rumpled top was a total distraction. Needless to say, she did not get the job.

A lot of people are led to believe that image only involves their outer appearance. Your physical presentation is only one segment of your image. The total reflection of yourself extends far beyond beauty, glamour, and being pretty or handsome. Your inner image (self-image) shapes your outer image. Self-image is your personal vision of yourself that is derived from a combination of your prior experiences, society, family, friends, internal thoughts, and beliefs. It is the reputation and relationship that you have with yourself. It echoes what we hold to be true about ourselves.

You are more than your looks. As an entrepreneur, you can have an amazing professional appearance, the most powerful mission statement, and the best branding, but if you are not crystal clear about your self-image and who you are, you will not reach your full potential and will possibly be viewed as insincere. Be cautious about the inner conversation that you allow to take place. This is the origin of your self-worth that spills over to your outer image. Make sure your self-talk is loving and gentle instead of harsh and cruel. Remember, this impacts your overall image—how you view yourself and what the world sees.

When it comes to your inner image, here are some things to consider. What does your self-image reflect? Is it negative or positive? A negative self-image emphasizes your weaknesses, while a positive self-image focuses on your strengths. The attitude that we choose to take is so important because the way we view ourselves directly impacts how we manage our lives. It all begins with loving and accepting ourselves for who we are.

Here are a several ways to improve your image:

- ❖ **Let your confidence shine:** When you walk into a room, be confident in your look and who you are. Confidence is attractive!

- ❖ **Speak positive words:** No one wants to be around Negative Norman or Debbie Downer. Great conversation will draw the right people to you in most situations.

- ❖ **Walk in purpose:** There is nothing more attractive than seeing a person authentically living out their purpose. Find what you are passionate about and go after it!

- ❖ **Try laughing more:** Loosen up and don't take life so seriously. Have fun and be free.

Others will see this in you and want to be in your presence.

❖ **Get rid of stress:** Don't wear stress, worry, and fear on your face. This a people repellent. Release all negative energy and maintain a peaceful state of mind.

❖ **Be authentically you:** Be comfortable in your own skin. Appreciate the uniqueness in yourself and others will follow suit.

❖ **Become the healthiest version of yourself:** Good health is the new wealth! Exercise, maintain a healthy diet, drink plenty of water, and be sure to get a sufficient amount of rest. When your body is healthy and fit, you look good and feel great!

❖ **Maintain your outer appearance:** Be sure to keep regular appointments with your hair stylist, a fresh manicure/pedicure, and a wardrobe that fits your personality.

Remember, image is everything, and it is essential to take pride in your appearance. Even if you went bankrupt and hit rock bottom, it doesn't mean you have to look like it. Just because you've been through a traumatic divorce, you do not have to carry that in your spirit for the rest of your life. Through my experiences I've learned that there will be many ups and downs…and trust me, I have had my share of downs. Not only is failure a part of life, but the ability to get up and start over is part of success. Because I know who I am and whose I am, I have learned to always dress as if I am prepared for my father's abundance. In other words, don't dress for where you are, but dress for where you are headed. When you look better you feel better, and when you feel better, you do better. Your image embodies your mind, body, and spirit. So, when you commit to having an amazing inner and outer image, you will begin to attract the things you desire into your life.

✓ **Transformational Tip:** Turn your Mess into a Masterpiece by indulging in self-care on a regular basis, and always show up looking your best.

CHAPTER 7: BE HAPPY

Enjoy the journey

When all is said and done, I think everyone just wants to be happy. To live life without constant confusion, chaos, or madness, but in a state of pleasure, contentment, joy, and peace, is what most wish for. Happiness is that feeling you get when deep down in your soul you know that life is good. By no means does it suggest that everything will be perfect in your life, but there comes a time that we must be responsible for our own happiness. Being happy is a choice. If you are sitting around hoping, wishing, and waiting for someone to fix you or save you, simply put, you are wasting your time. You have the power to change the course of your life. It doesn't matter who hurt you, who abandoned you, or what they said about you. What matters most is this moment that you have right now to use what you learned from your setbacks to live your best life and be happy.

There was a time in my life that I wasn't happy. I allowed every hardship that I had gone through to put me in a dark place. Honestly, I pretended to be cheerful when others were around, but my spirit and mind were unsettled. I just wanted everything to be good again. Day in and day out I would reflect on the success that I previously had in business and the lavish lifestyle I lived at that time. The more I held on to the past, the more miserable I became. I was walking in the store one day, and a gentleman passed by me and said, "Sister, don't be so mad." What was he talking about? As I quickly studied myself, I discovered that I was frowning for no reason. The inner turmoil had seeped into my outer expressions and I didn't even realize it. At that moment, I knew I had to do something different. Although things were not the way they had been, I had so much to be grateful for. From that point forward, not matter what state I was in, I decided to enjoy the journey and be happy.

Here are several things that you can implement in your daily life to facilitate a happy lifestyle:

- ❖ **Dream again:** One of the best things you can do is to awaken the dreamer in you. Don't fall for the lie that it's too late, you are not good enough, or too many people are already doing that. All things are possible.

- ❖ **Live with intention:** Wake up every day being deliberate about how you live. Gone are the days of merely accepting what happens. Have a strategy for your life and be intentional. This will give you a consistent focus and a greater sense of purpose.

- ❖ **Love again:** If you have truly healed from the hurts of past relationships, be open to share your heart with someone again. Now that you are better and not bitter, let love have its way.

❖ **Do things you enjoy:** It's okay to treat yourself to something nice. Whether it is shopping, a massage, a manicure, having brunch with a friend, reading a good book, or catching a movie at the theater, enjoy your life and have fun!

❖ **Don't sweat the small stuff:** Sometimes things are not as important as they may seem. If someone says bad things about you, brush it off. If you have one day of low sales in your business, don't major in the minors because tomorrow is a new day.

❖ **Stop trying to control everything:** If you are a control freak, stop it! There are some things in life that you don't have the power to change. Relax and let it go. Trust the process and know that everything will work out in its time.

❖ **Declutter and stay organized:** When your environment is in order, you tend to have organized thoughts and peace of mind. You will spend less time searching for things and avoid unnecessary frustration that often robs you of your peace.

❖ **Make yourself the priority:** Why spend your days taking care of and trying to please everyone else and neglect yourself? Remember, you set the best example of how others should treat you.

❖ **Manage your money wisely:** Financial struggle is one of the leading causes of stress and marital strain. Implement good money habits and wave your troubles goodbye.

❖ **Be a blessing to others:** Giving and helping others is one of the most rewarding things that you can do. Whether it is volunteering for a great cause or being there for a friend in the time of need, when you step outside yourself to do good for others, the satisfaction it brings is priceless.

❖ **Learn to say NO:** You can't be everybody's everything and that is okay. Eliminate false expectations by politely but clearly saying no as needed.

❖ **Get away:** Whether it is taking a few days off or simply enjoying your weekends, a nice getaway is often in order. Retreat to restore. You deserve it!

❖ **Just be yourself:** You don't have to prove yourself to anyone. You don't have to pretend to be something that you are not. Be free. Don't force it, no pressure, no pretending. Just be your true and authentic self.

✓ **Transformational Tip:** Dream!!! Life is too precious to live with regret. Go for it and enjoy the journey.

CONCLUSION

Remember, you are the captain of your ship and the master of your own life. You have the power to shift your world from Mess to Masterpiece. Leave the past behind you. It's a new day. Know that you are AMAZING and you don't have to look like what you've been through. There is greatness on the inside of you that is just waiting to burst out. It's time to look better, feel better, and be better. It is possible. The choice is yours. You can turn your Mess into a Masterpiece. Get ready to shine!

Available in Print, eBook and AudioBook!

Made in the USA
Middletown, DE
04 December 2019